Hello! [illegible] and I want to tell you [illegible] stories about our Gur[illegible] was our first Guru or teacher, Guru Gobind Singh was our tenth Guru. They lived in the Punjab, in northern India, many years ago.

The Potter's Donkey

All day long in the hot sun, the potter's donkey had to carry large sacks full of heavy pots through the market streets of Anandpur.

Guru Gobind Singh felt sorry for the poor animal. "If he had been born a tiger," thought the Guru, "his life would be very different." Then he had an idea!

The Guru untied the donkey and placed the tiger skin which he had been carrying, over the donkey's back.

Covered by the tiger skin, the donkey strolled through the market streets, eating everything he wanted from the stalls around him. He was having a wonderful time!

But when the stallholders saw him, they started to shout, "Help! Help! A tiger!" Some started to bang loudly on tins and drums to try and drive the tiger away!

The poor donkey was terrified. He began to turn round and round in circles ... and then he started to bray, "Ee aw! Ee aw!"

The stallholders were astonished!

"It's not a tiger, it's only the potter's donkey," they said scornfully.

They were no longer afraid.

"Hey, donkey," they cried, "if you are wearing the skin of a tiger, you have to be brave!

If you look like a tiger, don't go behaving like a donkey!"

The poor donkey felt ashamed of himself and went to find his master.

Bhai Lalo, the Guru's True Friend

In the village of Aminabad lived a poor carpenter called Bhai Lalo.

Every time Guru Nanak came to the village, Bhai Lalo would cook him a simple meal of chapattis and vegetables and sit listening to the Guru's stories.

One day, Malik Bhago, a very rich and important man, sent his servant to Guru Nanak inviting him to a feast.

Guru Nanak politely refused and settled down to eat with Bhai Lalo.

Malik Bhago was angry – he sent another servant.
Again, Guru Nanak politely refused.

Malik Bhago came to Guru Nanak himself.

"Why do you stay and eat with a poor carpenter? I am a rich man. I can afford anything! I can give you a magnificent feast!"

Guru Nanak looked at Malik Bhago and quietly replied,

"Bhai Lalo is a poor man but he shares all the food he has with me. That is the sign of a true friend."

Malik Bhago hung his head in shame.

Bhai Ganaya, the Water Carrier

All through the day, the armies had been fighting a hard battle. Many men had died and many were lying on the ground injured.

At dusk, Bhai Ganaya filled the water bottle he carried around his neck and went out into the battlefield looking for men who had been injured. Some men were hardly moving but Bhai Ganaya gently poured drops of water into their mouths.

Just then, one of his fellow Sikhs saw what he was doing and called out, "Hey, stop! You're giving water to our enemies!"

Hearing the shouts, Guru Gobind Singh crossed the battlefield. "You've been helping our enemies. What have you to say for yourself?" he asked.

"I don't see friends and enemies," Bhai Ganaya replied. "I just see men who are injured, men in pain, men who need water, men who need my help."

Guru Gobind Singh looked kindly at Bhai Ganaya, "You are right," he said. "We should treat everyone equally. Everyone deserves our help. Bhai Ganaya, you are a true Sikh!"

Can you tell your favourite story about one of the Gurus and what he was trying to teach?

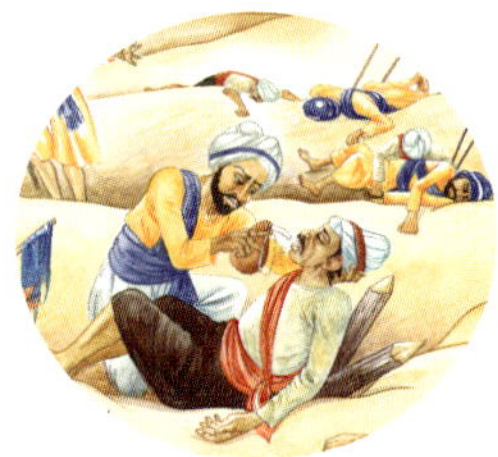

Published by RMEP (Religious and Moral Education Press)
An imprint of Hymns Ancient and Modern Ltd (a registered charity)
St Mary's Works, St Mary's Plain, Norwich, Norfolk NR3 3BH

First published 2009

ISBN 978-1-85175-431-1

Designed and typeset by Topics – The Creative Partnership, Exeter
Printed in Great Britain by Information Press, Eynsham, Oxford